1957

Bread Out of Stone

SCHARMEL IRIS

Drawn by Diego Rivera

SCHARMEL IRIS

BREAD OUT OF STONE

Preface by
WILLIAM BUTLER YEATS

Epilogue by
OLIVER ST. JOHN GOGARTY

HENRY REGNERY COMPANY
Publishers   *Chicago*

Acknowledgments

I gratefully acknowledge permission to include in this volume the poem "April" which first appeared in *The Little Review,* and thirty poems first printed in *POETRY: A Magazine of Verse* under the pseudonyms Wesley Ames, Stanley Blackpool, Everett Owens, and John Creagh. The remaining poems are published here for the first time.

The portrait reproduced in the frontispiece is the work of Diego Rivera, and was given to me by the artist, together with an oil painting, in return for a poem.

S. I.

Contents

· 3 ·

Preface

*A*fter they put a stone on the grave of Burns his mother was heard to cry out, "He asked for bread and ye gave him a stone!" For four decades Scharmel Iris sought bread in return for his poems but instead of bread the world cast him a stone. Somehow the rose that is crushed underfoot is the rose that gives us its perfume. He has made bread—bread out of stone—and we who have eaten of the bread have appeased our spiritual hunger.

I have carried the manuscript about with me for days, and I have often had to close it for the tears I could not stem. A French version of the "Old Courtezan" inspired the chisel of the immortal Rodin. Fired as he was by Sarah Bernhardt's reading the sculptor gave his statue that name.

Who can doubt that our history has been a history of violence, one dotted with bristling personalities? He seems so alien, like a voice of St. Francis—simple, orderly, burning with beauty and with a passion for perfection. All is near and dear to him. These qualities make these poems a pleasure and give weight to the poet's name. Of poets writing today there is no greater. What other poet could have written such a poem as "Pause during Rhythm"? It is a dark fire-filled gem, a gem of the first water. Certainly in "April" he has written one of the finest lyrics in the entire range of English literature. Poems like "Iteration" and "Lament" are great in that they are like a cry of the heart. That is all a poem can be. And when Sandburg called him "a genius in the lyric field" he expressed what other contemporaries have known since Francis Thompson said "his poems are worthy of the best poets." He has cast his net in the deep well of the spirit and has brought us Beauty naked and absolute. And he walks alone. He detests anthologies as much as I do. It means being paraded before the public with a lot of people to whom one hasn't been introduced. Browning said of his wife, "She likes being with the others," and added that he didn't.

Life has a way of striking blows. One of these blows was the theft of his poetical labours of some twenty years. Those "leaves in a dark wind" as he calls them are gone as his mortal body also must go. But this sheaf of poems slender as a woman's hand, shot with beauty as a star-filled sky, is indestructible; and shall remain forever what they are—a divine fire to light the way where once a poet breathed and lived and passed.

W. B. YEATS

Riverdale
Willbrook
Rathfarnham,
Dublin.
1934

April

J loved her more than moon or sun—
  There is no moon or sun for me;
Of lovely things to look upon,
  The loveliest was she.

She does not hear me, though I sing—
  And, oh, my heart is like to break!
The world awakens with the Spring,
  But she—she does not wake!

The Woman in the Wheat

I see the woman in the wheat
Cutting the grain she shall not eat.
The seven sons the woman bore
The king has sent to war.

The poppies in the wheat are blood,
And blood the crimson sunset-flood.
The Herod dawn a crimson hand
Has lifted over the land.

Within a shower of crimson rain
I see the woman in the grain.
The world is like a crimson sea
Between her heart and me.

On Cloth of Satin

Like a nude by Sorolla
See how she lies:
Warm amber on pink satin—
Beholder, feast your eyes!
Is there no surprise
For airs the flutes are playing
As they play in Paradise?
Suffer the roses, their falling petals,
Colored with lights from open skies.
Are your senses dulled that you do not see or hear
Sportive amoretti tumbling in mid-air;
The jewel-glow there
Where she lies:
Warm amber on pink satin
And she with welcoming eyes?

Hawks of Germany

Hear how they cry—
Not for the innocent whom they made die,
But for themselves, under a change of sky.

Razed, roof and nave,
Their square, squat temple which they could not save
With heavy arrogance, nor cheat the grave.

Hear how they cry,
The stubborn hawks that rent the quiet sky
With brimstone—these who know not how to die!

How Wonderful the Maid

How wonderful the maid
  When Christ of her was born!
Youthful and unafraid
  Of sharp encroaching thorn.

As sharp and clear the maid
  As were her lucid skies,
Wherein appeared to her
  All she need realize.

Old colors do not fade,
  Nor do old legends die.
How wonderful the maid
  Under a separate sky!

Shaken were all the stars
  By her one sleepy nod—
The maid that was fourteen,
  Come to deliver God.

The Old House

Largely adequate, remote, lofty as a mountain,
Father lived his Odyssey in this old house
Before his room was sealed to sunlight when he died,
A mid-Victorian room with prints by Piranesi.
Straight through the house ran the Damascus road,
Where, midway, mother had her homely vision
Of simple usefulness among her curlicues.
She laid aside her cloth of French rosettes,
Pottering with her children like a dotard in a garden,
Wise as the mother of the Gracchi and as exultant,
Pointing pride's sure finger toward her sons and daughters;
And passing on, smiled like a singing rainbow
Over a rain-drenched earth, a rainbow fixed above us.
Seven were buried from the old house.
O house untenanted, how like a breaking grounded ship—
The biting memory of you is like a wound of the heart!

A Poem

A poem is a magic thing—
It must be lucid, it should sing.
A cry that cuts the heart in two
Needs be true.
If it has a golden ring,
A poem is a magic thing—
It will sing.

Woman and Tree

A woman without son or daughter
Can come to peace by quiet water.
But the tyranny of beauty
In slow and glorious change,
Can well turn her strange;
Can leave her like a blackened stone
From which all force and fire have flown.

A golden tree can be a burning myth
And she a fabled monolith
In a pointed leaf and flower
Challenging hour.

Under an oriental sky of arrowy birds,
A woman without son or daughter
Can know the bite of gall, go empty of words;
The wild plum in delicate, ghostly bloom,
Drive her to doom.
Oh! desolate day
When walls fall at a cry
And exiled towers sway.

A speechless, wonderful, fruited tree
    Reflected in clear water,
Is a beautiful, terrible thing to see
    For a woman without son or daughter.

Against Gods

The shining laureled gods
  Scorn us in their mirth—
I am a strong tree risen
  Straight from the earth.

I will defy the gods,
  Affront them in their prattle.
Cleanly in my pride,
  Straight into battle.

My shout has split the dark
  Like a peacock's cry;
My heel a brand of fire—
  Now I can die!

The Blind

The chinless men wore beards,
The mountain held aloof.
Curious
How the blind wear spectacles.

The mountain humped its back
For the glint of God's foot,
Washed with stars.

In the valley miasma
The bearded men went,
Lame from gold.
Their beards sinned against Moses,
John the Baptist,
Christ.

They say we are poor, Lord,
Yet we thank Thee
For the gift of sight
And the great gift, hunger.

After Parting

If only I might rest!
   There is no peace in dying—
Over the storm-swept sea
   A gull is crying.

I am the storm-swept sea,
   The gull that cries alone;
There is no peace in dying—
   Girl, turned stone.

One-room Apartment

Her parrot, in its lacquered cage,
Is screeching in a scarlet rage.
In sparkling water, purpling-dim,
Her bright prismatic goldfish swim.
Before her glass she preens herself
And sees blue china on a shelf.
Dancing, she hums a jazzy tune,
And kicks her slipper to the moon.

Paganini

You pizzicato tease!
Grandmothers called you *diavolo*—
The devil is the other face of God.

Your bow of horse-hair charmed the moon,
The veiled and blushing moon.
Yes, you loved the moon as only poets love her—
Did she not dance for you on the ethereal blue waters at a
     carnival in Venice?

Your fiddle of tunes sleeps in a museum.
Dust lies on your bow.
In the cool sarcophagus of the earth your heart is a bundle
     of dust.

Yet, in many a garden of happy children is a clapping of
     petal hands
At your somersaults, spirals and confetti.

Lamentation

In pride our son stepped up to meet his death,
And is the earth's. O earth, most jealous mother!

Our light is now no more,
The path of the sun is creped with ravens;
Empty is the land,
And my heart is a pendulum of stone.

For he who moved among the maidens bright with youth,
Bronzed with the sun of summer,
Goes no longer among them,
But sleeps in a grass-thatched house.

Gargoyle Night

*F*ire lights the iconed wall,
  The cactus on the table;
Upon a gargoyle night like this
  Cain slew Abel.

Your kiss the kiss Iscariot
  To hang me on the tree;
Your fist is glut with lucre
  From mine enemy.

Cold Rain

I hear the tapping of a cane—
It is the blind man in the rain.
My room is like a mellow lyre
With bursting embers spitting fire,
And glint and glow in glass and lamp
And soft rugs like a Persian's camp.
God's pity be on bird and beast,
And beggars peering at a feast!
The bird is sleeping in his cage;
Untroubled is the dreaming sage—
Out with the blind man in the rain
My heart is beating like his cane.

On Fawns

*F*awn, in your leaping,
   Thunder assault!
They would make you Christian
   With a pinch of salt.

Stamping defiance,
   Flashing horns—
They would nail you on a cross
   Crowned with thorns.

He who would undo a fawn
   Wields the sword of treason.
Thunder your defiance—
   A fig for their reason.

Flowering Night

The sky hurls down a hundred stars
  Above a lake of amethyst;
Beyond the blooming lilac hills
  Wanders a thin blue mist.

This beauty is too great that one
  Should bear it all alone;
The night has flowered as has flowered
  My heart that was a stone.

Stone

*W*alking through grass I come on basic stone—
Free of summoning,
How good to be alone!

Stone, cold and clean, can be a chiseled flower—
Can stir remembrance
Like orchard blossoms' shower.

The ebbing grass cannot obscure calm stone
That gained in darkness
The strength which it has known.

The sustenance of strength is rooted deep—
Pregnant of a past
That has no tears to weep.

Pause During Rhythm

On a grape-colored hill
Against a greying sky
Blue-flame,
Florescent,
Your heels have cooled on fandangos.
Let fall your shawl—
Your rose-fuchsia, wine-petunia shawl.
Let your hair fall
Over the feet of Christ.
You have no need of lilies, virgin.
And do your eyes, luminous with tears,
Search still for the last, lost glint of grace?

Exultation

J have molded a chalice like thy breast,
O thou ivy-crowned!
In a secret niche thou art set apart.
Glamour falls upon thee like a cloak.
Thou art raised above the reach of kings,
And thou art sealed to me as the crocus is to Spring.

I sing thee in strange places till the old men snarl:
"He is drunk with sun!"

I go into the darkness singing—
Lips that have known thee taste not death.

Murderer

Jack has climbed my beanstalk.
At the bone-swinging
I shall drop Cain's hand-towel.

Thick-lipped Herod,
Rat-eyed Nero,
All had beanstalks;
All were midgets alongside our
Illustrious King of Coin,
Saint of the four halos—
Religion, Science, Education, Business.

Borgia poured thick wine—
The insatiable entertainer!

Villon had no pretenses;
Besides, he needed leisure for song-making.
The rest wore gloves,
Cheats at Pilate's wash-basin.

Jack has climbed my beanstalk.
At the bone-swinging
I shall drop Cain's hand-towel.

Tears

*U*pon the night that Christ was born
   He made a woman cry;
And cry again, when on the cross,
   They raised Him to the sky.

Tears, scalding tears, and tears that flow
   For every mother's son!
Mother of Judas, mother of Christ,
   Shed tears when it was done.

The Steel Hand

O comrade, flash your teeth at time!—
Though hands and face are smeared with grime.
Your sinews' and your muscles' ire
Passes like molten steel through fire.
What steel is there that can defy
The mastering steel within your eye?
But oh the conflict, stress and ache
Of flesh and spirit and heartbreak!
Your soul's bright steel through flame and dust
Laughs undismayed at conquering rust.

The Wild Plum Tree

I will not stay in the town
  Where laughter is too free.
Give me the wild plum in bloom,
  And the blue untroubled sea.

I do not know why they frown,
  Or laugh when they see me.
I'd rather the wild plum's dazzle
  Than apples on a tree.

I cannot live in this town
  Nor let them laugh at me—
I, who planted the moon at the root,
  Of the wild plum tree.

The Thug

Cat-like,
I foot the night
Foolish as a fox.

We must crack skulls,
Black-jack.
The Romans did it with a thumb—
The king with a gesture.

That tiaraed dame in the opera cloak
Met King Edward:
Tonight she meets me.

Citizens,
His honor the judge,
Bends a religious knee-cap
And smells of incense—
You have faith indeed.

His palm itches—
I must grease it with gold.
Besides, his mistress desires a tour.

The gallows-tree
Is the roost of buzzards.
My jig is for the go-between.

Cat-like,
I foot the night
Foolish as a fox.

War-time Cradle Song

The king sent out your father to war
As once he sent my father before.
My wedding ring and the gold on my ear
Today have I bartered for bread, my dear.
The moon is dying, her throat is red,
The wind is crying, "Your father's dead."

The holy priest for saying a mass
Will take our gentle ox and our ass,
And we must give our cow away
To a man who digs the grave today.
The king has given us a reward—
A medal of bronze, and your father's sword.

Grain there is none on the granary floor.
The lean wolf, Misery, howls at our door—
Until I wake and cut off my hair.
My son, I will keep you strong and fair,
For soon you shall take your father's sword
And bring me the king's head for reward.

The Stone Left Standing

The woman I loved has stepped into silence;
Shut is the wood where the gods walked.
Still as the still leaves about me
I think of her who was both flame and frost to me.
Fallen is the house, and I the stone left standing—
Who will sing of her when I too am forgotten?

Your Neighbor and Mine

Her life was like her quiet dress,
Her burning soul a quenchless light.
Mothering her sisters and her brothers
Who cried for mothering in the night,
Mothering them she knew
Not if the sea was blue
Or the sun in the sky.
She who was like a light—
Like a thief in the night
Love passed her by.
But on the day she came to die
Death laid her quiet dress away.
The common room filled with the light
Of her bright soul. That night
The neighbors did not stoop to pray
Marvelling at the light.

Hill Shadow

I never see a lovely hill
  But see a shadow on its crest;
Sorrow nailed upon a tree
  With pierced and bleeding breast.

Sorrow nailed upon a tree,
  Mocked with cruel thorny crown—
I never see a lovely hill
  But two grieved eyes look down.

As Glass Is Splintered

Blue, ever so blue, the glow
Of winter light on snow
Unscuffed of deer or doe
Or tyrant wind. "I've dropped a bird!"
Cried the elated hunter. Heaven scowled. I spoke no word.
No other sound was heard
Except the sibilant bleeding of the bird.
Sealed in my throat the word
Endlessly bleeding—the hoarse, fiercely deferred
Unuttered unassailable word.

It was my heart, never the ear that heard
The red cry, the last cry of the red-crested fire-winged bird.
Because of the bright bird, peony-colored, swiftly slain,
And my held-back frozen denial of pain,
Dark went the day and brightened not again.
I remember it well and all too well I know,
The scalding blood of the bird hurriedly ate a hole in the
  snow.

The Beggar

Your head is like a dome
  Of yellowing ivory.
Your face is like a mask
  That baffling, cunningly
And subtly hides your soul.
Your palm is but a bowl
  Of coin-dropped charity.

Into the theatre
  The crowds swarm heedlessly
  In blatant finery,
  And only see
The dust-gray of your clothes,
  And the pencils that you sell
  In your evident hell.
Finding you I find
The color of your mind,
And smell as smell I must,
The scent of stars arising from your dust.

Pines and Sand

Like a dead child with folded hands is this ascetic sand—
Spring rain has startled these pines into emerald flame.
Walk with me here; doves nest here; do not withdraw your
     hand.
Speak! your words are as wine. Walk! jewel the air!
Let down your warm dark fragrant hair.
Slim flames, blown out, these pine needles drop, decay—
They lit the face of a god who glimmered and went away.

The field that was garnet fire, flares violet gray.
Graver than yellow this cool, ascetic sand,
Where once a god walked, glimmered, and went his way.
Do not begrudge me your hand.
Is it such a dangerous thing
For one so plain as I to feel like a king;
That a word can shake me and jewel the air
And joy run tingling from fingertips to roots of my hair?
Among these pines the glimmering god has left his breath.
Having known you who glimmered above all others,
How can I dwindle, know the tyranny of death!

Old Courtesan

Once were her joys
A spread of colored toys.
Now lenten ashes gray
Infest her day.
Her sunken eyes and breast
Her doom attest.
Unconsecrated host!
What Holy Ghost
Can bring forth light
From the bleared jungle of her night?

O tree abhorred!
O broken temple of the Lord,
Cursing the judgment of the sun!—
God pity you, as I do, piteous one.

The Old Man

I am old now,
I am very old.
The sleep has come upon me
And my words. Today
Have I given all away.
Nor will I join in the talk
Of the old men in the park,
Tapping their canes around the well.
I have forgotten many things
For I am old,
Being cloaked in twilight.
I will stuff my pipe with stars
And go to sleep.

The Glory and the Worth

Saints without labels walk the earth—
Not I, not I.
Music and song and lips that sigh
I love, and groaning boards heaped high.
Not mine the glory, nor the worth.

Saints without labels on this earth
Work, pray and sigh.
Not they, the Lord to crucify,
Avoid His face, and pass Him by.
Theirs be the glory, theirs the worth!

Admonition

The red lark twirls
Three bright notes.

The great hibiscus breaks flamboyant,
The gold boy of the sky is a laughing archer,
The moon is a shining runner among stars
And she that was my heart stirs in her dust.

Bury me to the east
Under three bright notes!

Mexican Cock

You, the Carthage that has not perished,
Knowing that hate and love lie close together;
That calm alone can stop the excited sea.
Thrice-crowing prescient cock
Before denial became the Rock.
No goose-cackler saving Rome
But lord of bantam, ceremonial as the sun,
Scarlet-crested colored curve of spangled feathers—
No male intruder, you!
Adored as any actor on a hieratic stage
Or as an ancient idol in a secret Mexican cave.

In This Hour

It will be said of them:
They died in their finest hour—
The youths who gave their blood
To hold one flower.

Selfless they gave their all
The root to fructify.
Blessed be they and the earth
Wherever they lie.

The lame, the halt, and the blind
Have need of Thy pity, Lord,
But not the eager of limb
Broken upon the sword.

Praised be youth forever,
Lay wreaths where they lie—
They died in their finest hour
Who chose this hour to die.

After the Martyrdom

They threw a stone, you threw a stone,
   I threw a stone that day;
Although their sharpness bruised his flesh
   He had no word to say.

But for the moan he did not make,
   Today I make my moan;
And for the stone I threw at him
   My heart must bear a stone.

A Young Girl

*H*er eyes are full of tears
In passing.
Her grace is the grace of a fawn.
The spear of woe pierced her heart
And left her heart a stone.
A reed is she in the wind,
A song that cries for remembrance.

Song Against Ease

We have tarried overlong among the nightingales.
Clink heels over a sea of heads;
Let quick javelins clash above red bridges;
Let bright shouts break the march of peacocks.

It was the roses that seduced us.
Let the music be stern,
And sharp be the dancing.

Like a flamingo
Let us ride sun-down to a fixed rhythm.

Death is a clean curve:
Leap swiftly into the silence.

Lament

Lady, your heart has turned to dust,
   Your wail is taken by the sea;
The wind is knocking at my heart,
   And will not let me be.

Your moaning smites me in my dreams,
   And I must sorrow till I die;
And I shall rove, and I shall weep,
   Till in the grave I lie.

The Rounding of the Wave

Ringed in the shadow of death,
The old men peer at one another,
And at the pigeons pecking grain,
Cock-sure, avid, iridescent.

Iridescent
In the aura of youth—
Firmly I come against them
Here in the half-light, grumbling.

They have loved life,
Like Joachim his fiddle:
Death be the coming of a friend,
The folding of a flower,
The rounding of a wave.

Death Is a Dark Bull

Turn back from me, dark Death—
    I fear your horns.
But not the long, long sleep,
    The good fight, or the thorns.

So best me not, dark Death—
    Stay far from me
Who, broken among thorns,
    Am smote with ecstasy.

Lament for the Sun-bright Lover

Swished in a toothèd wind, in a watery grave he lieth—
My lover with the sun-bright hair, whose strength was like
    Goliath.

I let my dark hair down like the branches of the willow;
Oh, I would lean on death as a sleeper on a pillow.

I gouge my two eyes clean and sear my face with fire,
The keening's rent my heart and the last string of my lyre.

I rend the bridal robe I would have worn tomorrow;
A torn leaf on the wind am I in my blind sorrow.

Iteration

*M*y son is dead and I am going blind,
And in the Ishmael-wind of grief
I tremble like a leaf;
I have no mind for any word you say:
My son is dead and I am going blind.

Scarlet Cloak

*M*y grief now wears a scarlet cloak
  For love is dead—
Love that was sturdy as the oak;
  My brow goes gaily garlanded,
  No ashes on my head.
Come any day, come any morrow,
My scarlet cloak will baffle sorrow.

The Rock

Over the curve of her breast
 Nine children saw
Eagles circle the sun,
Mountains rise from the sea.

Up from her pots and pans
And the clutch of hands,
She made the sky;
While he who ran free
Tripped against pebbles.

I have begun,
I, their son,
To polish pebbles
With star dust from her outspread hair—
She who made the sky,
She who grew to be god.

The Lonely

Only the lonely
  Among men have known
Strength for ascension,
  Sup from a bone.

Only the lonely
  Have known, understood
Isaiah and Buddha,
  Christ on the rood.

Burdened and lonely
  And blinded by light,
Broken by beauty,
  Walking the night,

A cry can undo them,
  Rend them like pain—
And Death, down a man,
  In the familiar lane.

Nicobar Shaw

The nightingale imprisoned in his veins
Gave up its song to social gains.
At sea, in awe
Among old rags and iron, screw and saw,
Lived Nicobar Shaw.

A reed in the wind of greed
He raced with others of his breed.
Nicobar Shaw's respectability
Stood firm as stands a tree;
Yet under thin veneer were teeth and claw,
Steaming human jungle topped by Tablets of the Law.

I Wander and Wonder

I wander and wonder and walk all alone
Who ask for some bread and am given a stone.
I wonder how Christ felt when He walked like me
And wandered and wondered and saw what I see.

He wandered and wondered and He a great king.
I wander and wonder on how He could bring
To have Himself crucified high on the tree,
And all for the love of a poor one like me.

Early Nightfall

$\mathcal{T}$he pale day drowses on the western steep,
The toiler faints along the marge of sleep;
Within the sunset-press, incarnadine,
The sun, a peasant, tramples out his wine.

Ah, scattered gold rests on the twilight-streams,
The poppy holds her scarlet purse of dreams;
Night, with the sickle-moon engarners wheat,
And binds the sheaves of stars beneath her feet.

Rest, weary heart, and every flight-worn bird;
The brooklet of the meadow lies unstirred;
Sleep, every soul, against a comrade breast,
God grant you peace, and guard you in your rest!

Epilogue

*W*hy have I not heard of Scharmel Iris before this? Because of the critics who are like eunuchs posing as authorities on procreation. They don't know a thing about it; neither do critics know anything about poetry. It takes a poet to appreciate poetry. They alone have the receiving sets that are attuned to brave translunary things. That is why, until Yeats became aware of Scharmel Iris, he was more or less unhailed. Yes; a poet can best appreciate poetry. And the greater the poet, the greater the appraisement. That is why Yeats, the greatest poet of his period, gives this poet the greatest praise.

Scharmel Iris has imagination, music and a firm sense of metre. He is sure of himself within the bounds he has set for himself; and you feel that he will not let you down. "Working within limitations," says Goethe, "reveals the master." His limitations are the ballad metres of English poetry, the metres most akin to the genius of the language; but, at the same time, the most difficult of all metres because of their simplicity. You must have something to say. There is no room for padding. Listen to this, which is as well turned as anything A. E. Housman, that master of terseness, wrote:

> Selfless they gave their all
> The root to fructify.
> Blessed be they and the earth
> Wherever they lie.

> The lame, the halt and the blind
> Have need of Thy pity, Lord,
> But not the eager of limb
> Broken upon the sword.

Praised be youth forever
Lay wreaths where they lie!
They died in their finest hour
Who chose this hour to die.

Take those last two lines and realize all that is said in them. Compare these with Gerard Manley Hopkins, who introduced the hiccough into English prosody, and it becomes apparent at once how much greater power Scharmel Iris has.

I have read some statements full of regrets that Iris has had to wait long for "recognition." What is recognition? Why should a poet expect to be as popular and as widely distributed as paraffin oil? Do not call the public in! They have not the organ by which poetry is apprehended. Limericks are more in their line. All a poet wants is "a little clan." It is all that the best have had. Let him see to it, however, that he leaves it "great verse." This is great verse:

"Before denial became the Rock"

It has the fundamental brainwork of greatness. But it is as small verse compared with his "Scarlet Cloak." Here he ascends beyond anything that can be described as verse to that which is limitless and as incomprehensible as the wandering notes of a lost kingdom, "the horns of Elfland faintly blowing." You hear sounds which the sensual ear can hardly discern. And that is the function of a poet.

Why after all should we bother ourselves about these masters of words whom we call poets, or "makers"? Because of what they make. Words have built Heaven and founded Hell. Without them there is neither God nor Devil nor human intelligence. Not a sound of that world which eye hath not seen and yet is our only hope out of the slaughter-house which we call this life. On poets we have to depend for a glimpse of what lies beyond the veil. And they get it by

· 61 ·

using words as electrons which build the baseless fabric of a universe of their own.

Into the family of the "makers" Scharmel Iris ought to be satisfied at being welcomed and enrolled.

OLIVER ST. JOHN GOGARTY

"LIKE A VOICE of St. Francis — simple, orderly, burning with beauty and with a passion for perfection. . . Of poets writing today there is no greater." Thus, in 1934, William Butler Yeats described the poems in this volume. For the story of how these poems and Yeats' Preface were lost during the intervening years, turn to the back cover of the book jacket.

Critical Opinions on Scharmel Iris

GEORGE BERNARD SHAW: "His book will be received by two continents. His poems are not echoes of dead poets; they glow with the fire he has given them."

CARL SANDBURG: "Scharmel Iris is a genius in the lyric field."

WILLIAM CARLOS WILLIAMS: "His poems are top rank. There are not many pieces of writing you can say that about today."

GEORGE SANTAYANA: "His poems have much feeling and strength, but above all, the authority we call beauty."

ROBERT MORSS LOVETT: "One of that brotherhood of genius, at war with poverty and wrong, which includes Villon, Marlowe, Verlaine."